SURROUNDED BY WRONG PEOPLE

SURROUNDED BY WRONG PEOPLE

ROHIT KANADE

Nine99 Innovation Lab (OPC) Private Limited

Introduction

Welcome, dear friend, to a journey that will navigate the intricacies of human connections, unveiling the profound impact they have on our lives. In this book, "Surrounded by Wrong People," we embark on a quest to unravel the mysteries of toxic relationships and discover the transformative power of surrounding ourselves with the right individuals.

In Chapter 1, We will delve into the depths of human interactions, uncovering the telltale signs of the toxic trap that ensnares us all too often. Together, we will learn to recognize these signs, empowering ourselves with the knowledge needed to break free from detrimental patterns and forge a path towards healthier, more fulfilling relationships.

But this journey is not one of mere observation. It is a call to action—a call to embrace the power of choice. In Chapter 2, we will explore the vital role of building a support network. We will uncover the art of selecting individuals who uplift, inspire, and foster our personal growth.

Moving forward, Chapter 3 invites us to nurture healthy relationships, revealing the key ingredients that form the foundation of meaningful connections. From trust to communication, empathy to respect, we will embark on a quest to cultivate relationships that flourish and bring out the best in both ourselves and others.

In Chapter 4, we confront the challenging task of detoxifying our lives—a process that demands courage and strength. We will explore the art of letting go of toxic relationships, understanding that it is only by releasing the negative influences that we can create space for positivity to thrive.

The journey continues as we embrace the power of positivity in Chapter 5. Here, we explore the profound impact of surrounding ourselves with encouragement and inspiration. We will uncover the transformative effects of a positive environment and the role it plays in shaping our lives.

Chapter 6 shifts our focus towards the red flags and boundaries that are essential in identifying toxic traits. We will navigate the intricate landscape of human behavior, empowering ourselves to establish healthy boundaries that safeguard our well-being.

Embracing diversity takes center stage in Chapter 7 as we expand our perspectives and embrace the richness of different experiences, cultures, and beliefs. With an open heart and an inquisitive mind, we will celebrate the beauty of our differences and discover the transformative power of inclusivity.

Chapter 8 presents an exhilarating quest: finding our tribe—the souls who resonate with our essence and share our passions.We will explore the art of connecting with like-minded individuals, creating a supportive community that nurtures our growth and amplifies our impact.

The journey takes an inward turn in Chapter 9, where we discover the key to healthy relationships: cultivating self-love. We will explore the profound impact of valuing ourselves, nourishing our souls, and embracing our worthiness.

Finally, in Chapter 10, we unleash the extraordinary power within us as we become positive influences, paying forward the love, kindness, and wisdom we have gained on our journey. We embark on a mission to inspire and uplift those around us, creating a ripple effect that reverberates far beyond our own lives.

So, my friend, buckle up for an adventure that will reshape the way you view relationships. Let this book guide you towards a life surrounded by the right people. Together, we will unlock the secrets of healthy relationships, transforming ourselves and those we touch along the way.

CHAPTER 2

The Toxic Trap: Recognizing the Signs

In the labyrinth of life, we often stumble upon unexpected challenges. Some of these challenges, however, come in the form of people who camouflage themselves as friends but turn out to be toxic influences. Like a trap set in the darkness, they lure us in with false promises, draining our energy and clouding our judgment. But within each challenge lies an opportunity for growth and self-discovery.

Imagine stepping into a captivating masquerade ball, surrounded by beautifully adorned masks hiding the true intentions of those around you. In this enigmatic dance, toxic individuals may be dressed as charismatic jesters or enchanting sirens, beckoning us towards their treacherous webs. Yet, it is our duty to decipher their hidden motives and recognize the warning signs that lie beneath their shimmering facades.

Toxicity, like a poisonous serpent, slithers into our lives slowly and cunningly. It may manifest in various forms, from subtle manipulation to outright hostility. These individuals often possess the uncanny ability to drain our vitality, leaving us feeling empty and doubting our self-worth. They thrive on sowing seeds of negativity, fostering an environment where doubt and insecurities flourish.

Recognizing the signs of toxicity requires keen observation and introspection. It involves peeling back the layers of illusions and listening to the whispers of our intuition. Are their words laced with passive-aggressive undertones? Do they consistently disregard your boundaries, dismissing your needs and desires? These are the telltale signs of a toxic presence, a warning sign that you are waltzing on the edge of a perilous cliff.

However, it is essential to remember that we are not victims of circumstance. We hold the power of choice within our hands, capable of breaking free from the toxic bonds that ensnare us. Just as a spider weaves its web, we can spin a support network that empowers and uplifts us. It is through this web of genuine connections that we find solace and strength.

By forging relationships with individuals who inspire us, who genuinely care for our well-being, we construct a fortress against the toxicity that seeks to infiltrate our lives. These individuals become beacons of light, guiding us out of the darkness and into a realm of possibility and growth. They offer a listening ear, a helping hand, and unwavering support, nurturing the seeds of self-discovery that lie within us.

Detoxification of our lives requires a conscious effort to let go of toxic relationships that no longer serve us. Just as a skilled gardener prunes away dead branches to allow for new growth, we must rid ourselves of the negative influences that hinder our progress. It is a courageous act, for it requires us to confront our fears and confront the discomfort of change. But in doing so, we create space for positivity to flourish.

In the midst of toxicity, we must learn to navigate the treacherous waters with grace and resilience. It is not an easy task, but by recognizing the signs and making conscious choices, we begin the transformative journey towards freedom. Remember, the path to a healthier, more fulfilling life starts with acknowledging the toxic trap and mustering the courage to break free. So, put on your dancing shoes and take the first step—away from toxicity and towards a future where you are surrounded by the right people, who embrace your true worth and celebrate your journey of self-discovery.

CHAPTER 3

The Power of Choice: Building Your Support Network

Life is an intricate tapestry woven with the threads of our choices. With each decision we make, we shape the fabric of our existence. And when it comes to the people we surround ourselves with, we hold the brush that paints the portrait of our support network. Building a support network begins with a clear understanding of our own values, dreams, and aspirations. These are the guiding stars that illuminate our path, helping us to identify those who share our passions and align with our vision.

Now, building a support network doesn't mean seeking out clones of ourselves, for it is through diversity that we truly thrive. Surrounding ourselves with individuals who bring different perspectives, skills, and backgrounds to the table enriches our lives in immeasurable ways. It's like having a palette of vibrant colors to paint with, creating a tapestry that celebrates our differences and expands our horizons.

The beauty of choice lies not only in selecting who enters our support network but also in being mindful of who we choose to distance ourselves from. Toxicity, like a stubborn stain on a canvas, can mar the beauty of our lives. It is crucial to recognize the warning signs and disentangle ourselves from relationships that drain our energy, hinder our growth, and stifle our dreams.

Building a support network is an art form that requires both patience and courage. It starts with reaching out to those who inspire us, who radiate positivity and share in our joys and struggles. These individuals become the pillars of strength we can lean on when the winds of life blow fiercely. They offer a listening ear, a comforting presence, and unwavering encouragement when we need it most.

However, building a support network is not a one-way street. Like a dance, it requires both giving and receiving. Just as we seek support, we must also be willing to offer it in return. By being a trusted confidant, a source of empathy, and a cheerleader for others, we create a reciprocal bond that fosters growth and nurtures resilience.

In the art of building a support network, we must remember that quality trumps quantity. It is not about collecting an extensive roster of superficial connections but rather about cultivating deep, meaningful relationships. True support transcends social media numbers and popularity contests. It lies in the genuine connection we share, the mutual respect we hold, and the unwavering belief in each other's potential.

Building a support network is akin to assembling a mosaic, piece by piece. Each connection adds a unique color and texture to the overall picture of your life. Some may bring wisdom and guidance, while others may offer laughter and lightheartedness. Together, they form a beautiful collage that reflects the multifaceted nature of your journey.

In this process, be open to serendipity and unexpected encounters. Sometimes, the most profound connections come from the most unlikely places. Engage in activities and communities that align with your interests and passions, and let the universe weave its magic. You never know when you might stumble upon a soul that resonates deeply with your own.

It's important to remember that building a support network isn't about relying solely on others for your happiness or success. Rather, it's about creating a space where you can both give and receive support, where you can share your dreams and struggles, and where you can grow together. It's a reciprocal dance, a beautiful exchange of energy and understanding.

As you venture further into the realm of building your support network, you may encounter challenges along the way. Not every connection will be a perfect fit, and that's okay. Trust your intuition and be willing to let go of relationships that no longer serve your growth and well-being. Surround yourself with people who lift you up, challenge you to be your best self, and remind you of your inherent worth.

And amidst all of this, never forget the most important relationship of all—the one you have with yourself. Nurture self-love and self-care, for they are the foundation upon which all other connections are built. Take time to listen to your own needs, dreams, and desires. Treat yourself with kindness and respect, and in doing so, you will attract individuals who mirror those qualities back to you.

So, dear friend, as you continue to navigate the intricacies of building your support network, embrace the power of choice. Select those who bring out the brilliance within you, who see your potential even when you doubt it yourself. Together, you will forge a network that strengthens, uplifts, and nourishes your soul. And with this newfound support, you will be able to overcome any obstacle, chase your dreams, and bask in the radiant light of a community that truly believes in you.

CHAPTER 4

Nurturing Healthy Relationships: The Key Ingredients

In the vast garden of human connections, we find ourselves surrounded by a tapestry of relationships, each one unique and deserving of tender care. Like a skilled chef crafting a masterpiece, we must gather the key ingredients that nurture healthy bonds and cultivate a flourishing garden of love, trust, and understanding.

The first ingredient is communication— the seasoning that brings flavor and depth to our relationships. It is through open, honest, and compassionate dialogue that we bridge the gaps between hearts and minds. As we listen attentively, share our thoughts sincerely, and seek to understand rather than to judge, we lay the foundation for a connection built on authenticity and mutual respect.

Next, we sprinkle in the essential spice of empathy. This magical ingredient allows us to step into the shoes of another, to feel their joys and sorrows, and to offer a comforting presence when they need it most. Empathy helps us create a safe space where vulnerability is cherished, and compassion flows freely. It is the elixir that fosters deep bonds and paves the way for meaningful connections.

Now, let's not forget the pinch of trust. Like the binding agent that holds a recipe together, trust is the cornerstone of healthy relationships. It is earned through consistency, reliability, and integrity. We build trust by honoring our commitments, respecting boundaries, and showing up with authenticity. Trust is the glue that holds hearts together, allowing us to rely on one another and weather the storms of life as a unified force.

As we stir our relational concoction, we mustn't neglect the sweet ingredient of appreciation. A little sprinkle of gratitude goes a long way, my friend. Acknowledging and celebrating the unique qualities, talents, and contributions of our loved ones nourishes their spirits and strengthens the bond we share. Let us savor the beauty in their presence, expressing our gratitude for the joy and growth they bring into our lives.

Ah, and what feast of healthy relationships would be complete without the generous serving of boundaries? Yes, boundaries are the wise chefs in our kitchen, ensuring that each ingredient is given its proper place and proportion. By setting clear boundaries, we protect our emotional well-being, honor our own needs, and allow others to do the same. Boundaries are the recipe for harmony, fostering healthy interdependence and preserving the sanctity of our individuality.

Now, as our relational masterpiece simmers, we sprinkle in the secret ingredient: time. Relationships, like fine wine, grow richer and more nuanced with the passage of time. We must invest our precious moments, nurturing and tending to the connections that matter most. Quality time spent together, shared experiences, and heartfelt conversations all deepen the bonds that form the bedrock of our support and love.

And as we savor the fruits of our labor, we come to understand that healthy relationships are not stagnant but ever-evolving. They require ongoing care, attentiveness, and a willingness to adapt and grow together. We must be flexible in our expectations, patient in our understanding, and forgiving in our hearts. Our relationships thrive when nurtured with love, patience, and resilience.

But let us not forget the vital ingredient of forgiveness. Like the balm that heals wounds, forgiveness allows us to release the weight of past hurts and embrace a future filled with compassion and growth. It is a gift we give ourselves and others, liberating us from the chains of resentment and opening the door to renewed connection. Forgiveness is not a sign of weakness, but a courageous act of love that paves the way for healing and reconciliation.

Finally, we must cherish the importance of quality over quantity in our relationships. Like savoring a decadent dessert, let us focus on the depth and richness of our connections rather than the sheer number of acquaintances. It is the depth of our relationships that brings true fulfillment and nourishment to our lives. Surround yourself with those who uplift and inspire you, those who reflect your values and aspirations. Choose quality over quantity, and your relationships will be a source of strength and joy.

So, as you embark on the journey of nurturing healthy relationships, remember the key ingredients: communication, empathy, trust, appreciation, boundaries, time, and forgiveness. May your connections be as satisfying and nourishing as the most delightful feast. And may your life be graced with an abundance of love, support, and deep connection. Bon appétit!

CHAPTER 5

Detoxifying Your Life: Letting Go of Toxic Relationships

Picture This: you are strolling through a beautiful garden, filled with vibrant blooms and fragrant blossoms. But amidst the beauty, there are some weeds that threaten to overshadow the splendor. These weeds, my friend, are the toxic relationships that entangle us in their grasp. They drain our vitality, distort our perceptions, and stifle our true potential. It's time to put on our gardening gloves and free ourselves from their suffocating grip.

Recognizing a toxic relationship is the first step in this liberating process. Just as a skilled detective uncovers hidden clues, we must sharpen our senses to discern the red flags. Is there constant negativity, manipulation, or disrespect? Are your needs consistently disregarded, while the other person's desires take center stage? Trust your intuition, for it is a powerful compass guiding you toward healthier shores.

Letting go of toxic relationships can be daunting, for we may fear the unknown and the void it leaves behind. But remember that by releasing what no longer serves us, we create space for new, positive energies to enter our lives. It is like decluttering a room, creating an inviting space for fresh air and sunlight to flood in. Trust that as you let go of toxic relationships, you are making room for healthier connections to flourish.

Detoxifying your life requires strength and courage, for it often means setting boundaries and saying goodbye to those who drain your vitality. Remember, boundaries are not walls; they are loving barriers that protect your well-being. By establishing clear boundaries, you send a powerful message to the universe that you deserve respect, love, and positivity in your relationships.

As you embark on this journey of detoxification, surround yourself with a support network that champions your growth. Seek solace in the company of friends and loved ones who uplift your spirit and nourish your soul. Their unwavering support will serve as a beacon of light, guiding you through the sometimes tumultuous process of letting go.

And amidst it all, be gentle with yourself. Detoxification takes time, patience, and self-compassion. Allow yourself to heal, to grieve the loss of what once was, and to embrace the freedom that comes with releasing toxic ties. Treat yourself with kindness and nurture your soul as you create a life filled with authenticity, positivity, and genuine connections.

Detaching from toxic relationships is an act of self-love, not selfishness. It is a courageous step toward reclaiming your power and honoring your worth. Embrace the liberation that comes with letting go, and trust that you are creating space for the right people, the ones who will uplift, support, and cherish you as you deserve.

So, Remember to tend to your garden of relationships with care. Weed out the toxic influences, nurture the bonds that bring you joy and fulfillment, and create a sanctuary where love, respect, and positivity can thrive. Detoxify your life, and watch as you blossom into the radiant, empowered individual you were always meant to be.

Take a moment to reflect on the patterns and dynamics that kept you entangled in toxic relationships. Was it a lack of self-worth, fear of loneliness, or the belief that you didn't deserve better? This introspection allows us to gain clarity and recognize our own role in perpetuating these harmful connections. It is through self-reflection that we can break free from the cycle and pave the way for healthier relationships.

Detoxifying your life is not just about letting go; it is also about nourishing your own well-being. Prioritize self-care and self-love as you create a life that aligns with your values and aspirations. Engage in activities that bring you joy, practice mindfulness to cultivate inner peace, and surround yourself with positivity in all aspects of your life.

And as you navigate this transformative process, becoming your most authentic self is a gift not just to yourself but also to the world. By breaking free from toxic relationships and embracing your true essence, you inspire others to do the same. Your journey becomes a beacon of hope and empowerment, illuminating the way for others who may be caught in the toxic trap.

In the end, detoxifying your life from toxic relationships is not just about surrounding yourself with the right people; it is about becoming the right person for yourself. It is about embracing your worth, nurturing your dreams, and creating a life filled with love, respect, and positivity. Draw strength from within, lean on your support network, and trust in your own resilience. Embrace the freedom that comes with detoxifying your life, and step into a future filled with genuine connections, personal fulfillment, and boundless possibilities.

CHAPTER 6

Embracing Positivity: Surrounding Yourself with Encouragement

Just as the warm rays of the sun infuse the world with brightness, so too can positivity illuminate our lives and transform our relationships.

Imagine a garden bursting with vibrant flowers, their colors dancing in harmony with the gentle breeze. Positivity, my friend, is like the nectar that nurtures these blooms, infusing our lives with a sense of hope, joy, and resilience. It is the magnetic force that attracts like-minded souls and fosters an environment where love and encouragement thrive.

In a world that can sometimes seem clouded by negativity, embracing positivity becomes a conscious choice—a decision to surround ourselves with people who uplift and inspire us. Seek out those who radiate optimism, who see possibilities even in the face of adversity. Their infectious energy will invigorate your spirit and ignite a flame of hope within you.

But let us not mistake positivity for blind optimism or the denial of life's challenges. It is not about plastering on a smile in the midst of turmoil or avoiding the reality of difficult situations. Instead, it is a mindset—a lens through which we choose to view the world, recognizing that even in the darkest of times, there is a glimmer of light and an opportunity for growth.

Surrounding yourself with encouragement is a key element of embracing positivity. Seek out individuals who believe in your potential, who celebrate your successes, and who lift you up when you stumble. Their unwavering support becomes a safety net, allowing you to take risks, chase your dreams, and soar to new heights.

Let us not forget that positivity begins within. Cultivate self-talk that is kind and affirming. Celebrate your own achievements, no matter how small, and acknowledge the progress you've made on your journey. Your self-belief will radiate outward, attracting positivity and inspiring others to do the same.

As you navigate the path of positivity, be mindful of the energy you bring to your relationships. Are you a source of light and encouragement for others? Do you offer words of praise and appreciation, sprinkling seeds of affirmation wherever you go? Embrace the power of uplifting those around you, for in doing so, you create a ripple effect that touches lives far beyond your own.

Also, let us not forget the transformative nature of gratitude in nurturing positivity. Like a gentle breeze that caresses your skin, gratitude invites us to pause and appreciate the blessings that surround us. Take a moment each day to reflect on the things you are grateful for—the beauty of nature, the warmth of a loved one's embrace, or the simple joys that bring a smile to your face. Gratitude shifts our focus from what is lacking to what is abundant, infusing our lives with a sense of fulfillment and contentment.

Embracing positivity also means finding the silver linings in life's challenges. Adversity may knock on our door, but it is in those moments that we discover our own strength and resilience. Embrace the lessons learned from difficult experiences and let them shape you into a wiser, more compassionate individual. Embrace the belief that every setback is an opportunity for growth and that you have the power to overcome any obstacle.

In the pursuit of positivity, let go of comparison. Each of us is on a unique journey, and our paths unfold at their own pace. Embrace your own growth and progress, celebrating the milestones you've achieved. Remember that comparison steals joy and robs you of the present moment. Embrace your own journey, and let positivity blossom from within.

Lastly, let kindness be your guiding light. Acts of kindness not only uplift others but also bring immense joy and fulfillment to your own life. Extend a helping hand, offer a listening ear, or simply share a smile with a stranger. The ripple effect of kindness is immeasurable, spreading positivity far and wide.

As you continue to embrace positivity, remember that it is a lifelong journey, a daily practice of cultivating and nurturing the light within you. Embrace the challenges that come your way as opportunities for growth, and choose to see the beauty in every experience. Surround yourself with positivity, anchor yourself in gratitude, and radiate joy to the world.

CHAPTER 7

Red Flags and Boundaries: Identifying Toxic Traits

Let us dive into the intriguing realm of red flags and boundaries—a dance of self-awareness and assertiveness that empowers us to identify and navigate the treacherous waters of toxic relationships. Picture yourself as a skilled detective, equipped with a sharp wit and an unyielding commitment to your own well-being.

It is essential to develop the keen ability to spot the telltale signs of toxicity. Just as a skilled sailor reads the changing winds and tides, we must learn to discern the subtle cues and behaviors that may indicate an unhealthy dynamic. From manipulative mind games to a consistent lack of respect, these red flags flutter like warning beacons, urging us to proceed with caution.

But fear not, for armed with knowledge, you possess the power to establish firm boundaries that safeguard your emotional well-being. Like a castle with impenetrable walls, your boundaries define the limits of what you are willing to accept and protect your inner sanctum from harm. They are the shield that guards your authenticity and the compass that guides you towards healthy connections.

Setting boundaries is an act of self-love and self-respect. It is about honoring your needs, desires, and values, and communicating them with clarity and grace. It requires the courage to assert yourself, to say no when necessary, and to assert your worth without apology. Boundaries are the gatekeepers of your emotional landscape, ensuring that only those who respect and uplift you are granted entry.

Recognizing toxic traits and establishing boundaries go hand in hand. By identifying the patterns and behaviors that drain your energy and compromise your well-being, you gain the power to protect yourself and cultivate relationships that nourish your soul. Toxicity can manifest in various forms—constant criticism, manipulation, lack of empathy, or a consistent disregard for your boundaries. As you become more attuned to these signs, you can navigate the vast sea of human connections with wisdom and discernment.

But let us not forget, that we too must examine our own actions and ensure that we do not unknowingly contribute to toxic dynamics. Self-reflection is the mirror that reveals our own shadows—the times when we may have unintentionally crossed boundaries or engaged in unhealthy behaviors. By holding ourselves accountable and cultivating self-awareness, we become agents of positive change and break free from the cycles of toxicity.

Navigating the delicate terrain of red flags and boundaries requires courage. It may mean stepping away from relationships that no longer serve your growth or having difficult conversations to assert your needs.

One valuable tool in our arsenal is the power of observation. Cultivate an attentive eye and pay close attention to the subtle cues and behaviors that may signal toxicity. Trust your intuition, for it is a compass that guides you towards what feels authentic and nurturing. Notice patterns of consistent disrespect, manipulation, or a persistent imbalance of power within your relationships. These telltale signs can serve as guideposts, urging you to reevaluate the dynamics at play.

Additionally, develop the skill of active listening. By truly hearing and understanding the words, actions, and emotions of others, you gain insight into their intentions and character. Listen not only to what is said, but also to what remains unspoken. Seek to comprehend their motivations, their attitudes towards boundaries, and their willingness to respect your needs. Active listening allows you to uncover hidden red flags and make informed decisions about the health of your relationships.

The journey of identifying toxic traits and setting boundaries is not a linear one. It is an ongoing process of self-discovery, growth, and adaptation. Be patient and compassionate with yourself as you navigate this terrain, for it takes time to develop the wisdom and resilience needed to create healthy, balanced relationships.

Remember, you are worthy of love, respect, and healthy connections. Embrace the discomfort of growth and trust that by letting go of toxic relationships, you make room for new, enriching connections to blossom.

CHAPTER 8

Embracing Diversity: Expanding Your Perspectives

In a world filled with vibrant colors and multifaceted souls, we embark on a journey that celebrates the beauty of our differences and unlocks the transformative power of embracing diversity.

Imagine a grand tapestry, woven together by threads of unique experiences, beliefs, and backgrounds. It is within this tapestry that we find the extraordinary richness of humanity. Embracing diversity is not simply about tolerating differences; it is about recognizing the inherent value and wisdom that each individual brings to the table.

Like an explorer venturing into uncharted territories, we venture beyond our comfort zones and immerse ourselves in the mosaic of cultures, ideologies, and perspectives. We expand our horizons, shedding the constraints of limited understanding and embracing the boundless potential of shared knowledge and collective growth.

At the heart of embracing diversity lies the recognition that our own worldview is but a tiny fragment of the greater tapestry. Each thread, each unique perspective, adds depth, vibrancy, and nuance to the masterpiece of human existence. We open our minds, our hearts, and our souls to the wisdom that comes from engaging with those whose experiences and beliefs differ from our own.

Yet, my friend, embracing diversity goes beyond mere tolerance; it requires genuine curiosity and a willingness to challenge our preconceived notions. It beckons us to step into the shoes of another, to listen with empathy, and to seek understanding even in the face of disagreement. Through this open-hearted approach, we foster an environment where true dialogue flourishes, paving the way for growth, unity, and harmony.

In this magnificent tapestry of diversity, we discover the power of interconnectedness. We find that our commonalities outweigh our differences, that our shared humanity unites us in ways that transcend borders, cultures, and traditions. It is through the celebration of diversity that we build bridges of understanding and forge connections that extend far beyond our own limited spheres.

Embracing diversity is not without its challenges.It requires us to confront our own biases and prejudices, to dismantle the walls of ignorance and fear that hinder our progress. It beckons us to question the status quo, to challenge societal norms, and to champion equality and justice for all.

Let us remember that embracing diversity begins within ourselves. It starts with a humble recognition of our own limitations, an acknowledgment that we are forever learners on the path of understanding. By cultivating an open mind and an open heart, we invite the wisdom and beauty of diverse perspectives into our lives.

In life, each thread represents a unique perspective, a story waiting to be heard. When we open our hearts and minds to embrace diversity, we invite a symphony of ideas, beliefs, and experiences to resonate within us. It is within this symphony that new possibilities emerge, as the collision of contrasting viewpoints sparks creativity and fuels transformative change.

Imagine a gathering of minds, each bringing their own kaleidoscope of insights and perspectives. In this vibrant exchange, ideas dance and intertwine, forming intricate patterns of innovation and discovery. It is through the inclusion of diverse voices that we unlock the full potential of human ingenuity, pushing the boundaries of what is known and ushering in a brighter, more inclusive future.

Embracing diversity nurtures empathy and compassion within us. As we connect with people whose experiences differ from our own, we gain a deeper appreciation for the challenges they face and the triumphs they celebrate. We learn to listen attentively, to suspend judgment, and to extend a hand of understanding. In doing so, we build bridges of empathy that span across cultural, social, and linguistic divides, fostering a sense of unity and shared humanity.

To truly embrace diversity, we must go beyond surface-level acceptance and engage in meaningful allyship. We must amplify marginalized voices, uplift underrepresented communities, and actively work towards creating inclusive spaces where everyone feels seen, heard, and valued. It is through our collective efforts that we can bring about lasting change and create a world where diversity is not only celebrated but also integrated into the fabric of our societal norms.

With a commitment to inclusivity and a thirst for knowledge, let us navigate the intricacies of diversity, creating a symphony of voices that celebrates the tapestry of humanity in all its breathtaking diversity.

CHAPTER 9

Finding Your Tribe: Connecting with Like-Minded Souls

Welcome to the captivating chapter where we embark on a quest to find our tribe, those like-minded souls who light up our world and fill our lives with joy, understanding, and a sense of belonging. In a vast sea of humanity, discovering our tribe is like finding that elusive puzzle piece that perfectly fits into the intricate mosaic of our lives.

Finding your tribe is not just about surrounding yourself with people who share similar interests or hobbies; it is about forging deep connections that resonate on a soul level. It is about finding those individuals who see you, who truly understand and accept you for who you are. They are the ones who inspire and uplift you, who encourage your dreams and cheer for your successes.

Picture a gathering of kindred spirits, a diverse ensemble of unique personalities united by a shared sense of purpose and a genuine connection. These are the individuals who effortlessly bring out the best in you, who challenge and inspire you to grow, and who celebrate your victories as if they were their own. In their presence, you feel seen, heard, and valued, knowing that you are an integral part of a larger tapestry.

But, finding your tribe requires an openness and willingness to explore. It entails venturing outside your comfort zone and embracing the serendipitous encounters that life presents. Sometimes, it may require a leap of faith, a daring step into the unknown, for it is in those moments of vulnerability that the most profound connections are often forged.

It's important to remember that your tribe may not necessarily be found in the most obvious places. They may be hiding in the unlikeliest of corners, waiting to be discovered. They could be found in a small community organization, a local club, or even in the online spaces that have become our modern-day meeting grounds. Be open to the unexpected, for your tribe may be just a conversation away.

In the search for your tribe, authenticity becomes your guiding light. Embrace your true self, unabashedly and unapologetically, for it is through authenticity that you attract those who resonate with your genuine essence. When you embrace who you are, you radiate a magnetic energy that draws in souls who align with your values, passions, and aspirations.

Yet, it's important to note that finding your tribe doesn't mean surrounding yourself with a homogeneous group of individuals. It's about fostering a diverse community where different perspectives are valued, and where growth and learning flourish. Your tribe can be a tapestry of diverse backgrounds, experiences, and beliefs, all united by a common thread of mutual respect and support.

As you embark on this exhilarating journey, be patient, for finding your tribe may take time. It's a process of exploration, self-discovery, and meaningful connections. Be open to the possibility of evolving relationships, for as you grow and change, your tribe may evolve with you. Cherish the connections that stand the test of time, and graciously release those that no longer align with your path.

Finding your tribe requires active participation and a willingness to invest time and energy into cultivating meaningful connections. Engage in activities and communities that align with your values and interests. Attend events, join clubs, and participate in discussions where you can meet individuals who resonate with your aspirations. Be open to forming bonds that transcend superficiality, for it is the depth of connection that will sustain you during both triumphs and tribulations.

When building your tribe, remember that quality surpasses quantity. It's not about accumulating a vast number of acquaintances, but rather about forging deep, genuine friendships. Cherish the connections that spark joy, inspire growth, and ignite your passions. These are the relationships that will endure the test of time, providing unwavering support and celebrating your journey as you do theirs.

Be mindful of the values and energy you bring into these relationships. Nurture an environment of authenticity, trust, and support. Encourage open and honest communication, and be willing to vulnerably share your thoughts and emotions. By cultivating these qualities within yourself, you create a space that attracts like-minded souls who are also seeking meaningful connections.

So, in the journey of finding your tribe, trust in the serendipity of life, embrace the diversity of human connection, and remain open to the profound impact these relationships can have on your personal development.

CHAPTER 10

Cultivating Self-Love: The Key to Healthy Relationships

In a world where external influences often seek to define our worth, it is essential to anchor ourselves in the deep reservoirs of self-acceptance, compassion, and appreciation.

Picture this: a garden brimming with vibrant flowers, each one unique and exquisite in its own way. Just as each flower requires nourishment, care, and sunlight to thrive, so too does our inner being require tender love and attention. Cultivating self-love is akin to tending to the garden of our souls, nurturing our innermost desires and embracing our flaws with kindness and understanding.

To truly love oneself is not an act of arrogance or self-indulgence, but a profound act of self-respect and acknowledgement of our inherent worthiness. It is about recognizing that we are deserving of love, compassion, and happiness, irrespective of external validations or societal expectations. Self-love is the foundation upon which healthy relationships are built, for how can we authentically love others if we have not first learned to love ourselves?

In the pursuit of cultivating self-love, it is crucial to silence the inner critic and banish the shadows of self-doubt. We must become attuned to the whispers of self-compassion and embrace our imperfections as integral parts of our unique tapestry. Remember that perfection is an illusion, and it is our vulnerabilities and quirks that make us beautifully human.

Self-love is not a destination but an ongoing practice—a dance of self-care and self-acceptance that requires consistent effort and nurturing. It involves setting healthy boundaries, honoring our needs, and prioritizing our well-being. It is about listening to the whispers of our hearts and honoring the desires that ignite our souls. Engage in activities that bring you joy, practice mindfulness to cultivate inner peace, and surround yourself with people who celebrate and uplift your authentic self.

In the pursuit of self-love, let us also extend the same compassion and understanding to others. For it is through empathy and acceptance that we create a ripple effect, nurturing a collective environment of love and support. By cultivating self-love, we become beacons of inspiration, inspiring those around us to embark on their own journeys of self-discovery and acceptance.

One of the key aspects of cultivating self-love is practicing self-care. This involves nourishing not only our physical bodies but also our minds and spirits. It means carving out time for activities that bring us joy and fulfillment, whether it's indulging in a favorite hobby, taking a leisurely stroll in nature, or simply curling up with a good book and a warm cup of tea. By prioritizing self-care, we send a powerful message to ourselves that we are deserving of love and attention.

Another crucial element in cultivating self-love is practicing self-compassion. We must learn to embrace our shortcomings and mistakes with kindness rather than self-judgment. Instead of berating ourselves for perceived failures, let us offer ourselves understanding and forgiveness. Just as we would extend compassion to a dear friend who is going through a challenging time, we should extend that same compassion to ourselves. Remember, dear reader, that we are all beautifully flawed and deserving of our own forgiveness.

Lastly, cultivating self-love is an ongoing practice that requires patience, persistence, and self-reflection. It is not a destination but a continuous journey of growth and self-discovery. There may be days when you stumble or falter, but each setback presents an opportunity for learning and resilience. Embrace the process, for it is through the challenges and triumphs that we truly come to know and love ourselves.

Remember that you are worthy of love, respect, and all the blessings life has to offer. Nurture the flame of self-love within you, and watch as it illuminates your path, attracting positive and uplifting relationships that align with your highest self.

CHAPTER 11

Becoming a Positive Influence: Paying It Forward

As we have journeyed through the pages of this book, delving into the depths of toxic relationships, self-discovery, and cultivating healthy connections, we now stand poised to embark upon an extraordinary mission—to radiate positivity and inspire those around us.

Paying it forward is a concept that transcends mere acts of kindness; it is an embodiment of our power to uplift, transform, and create a wave of goodness that can touch the lives of countless individuals. Imagine the immense impact we can make simply by extending a helping hand, offering a listening ear, or spreading words of encouragement. Our actions, no matter how seemingly small, have the potential to ignite a spark in others, unleashing a chain reaction of positivity that reverberates far beyond our immediate reach.

But how do we become such a positive influence, you may wonder? It begins with cultivating a genuine and compassionate mindset. It is about seeing the beauty and potential in every individual we encounter, and approaching them with empathy and understanding. By embracing a mindset of abundance rather than scarcity, we unlock a wellspring of generosity that flows freely, enriching not only the lives of others but also our own.

To become a positive influence, we must lead by example. Our actions speak volumes and they have the power to inspire and motivate those around us. It is through our own growth, resilience, and pursuit of personal fulfillment that we become beacons of hope and catalysts for change. By nurturing our own well-being and pursuing our passions, we demonstrate the transformative power of authenticity and purpose, inviting others to embark on their own journeys of self-discovery.

As we venture forth into the realm of becoming a positive influence, let us not underestimate the significance of our words. Our voices, when used wisely and thoughtfully, possess the ability to uplift, heal, and ignite a fire within others. By speaking words of encouragement, offering genuine compliments, and expressing gratitude, we create a harmonious symphony of positivity that reverberates through the hearts and minds of those we encounter.

Paying it forward also encompasses the power of collaboration and community. By joining forces with like-minded individuals, we amplify our impact and create a collective force for good. Together, we can initiate projects, campaigns, and initiatives that address social issues, promote equality, and uplift marginalized voices. Through collaboration, we tap into the strength of unity and create lasting change that extends far beyond our individual capabilities.

Let us go forth with open hearts and minds, ready to embrace the incredible journey of becoming a positive influence. Let us embrace the challenges and triumphs that lie ahead, knowing that each step we take towards becoming a positive influence brings us closer to a world brimming with love, understanding, and harmony. Remember that our journey is not about seeking recognition or accolades; it is about the genuine desire to make a difference, however small or significant.

So, I invite you to embrace the profound power within you to become a positive influence. Let your light shine brightly, radiating love, kindness, and compassion. In doing so, you will not only transform the lives of others but also create a ripple effect that extends far beyond what you can imagine.

Remember, my dear friend, that you have the power to shape your own narrative, to forge connections that nurture your soul, and to create a life filled with love, joy, and purpose. I wish you the utmost success in your pursuit of healthy relationships, and may you forever be surrounded by those who lift you higher and inspire you to become the best version of yourself.